Cinéma Vérité

Works by Sam Rasnake

Necessary Motions

Lessons in Morphology

Tales of Brave Ulysses (Series)

Religions of the Blood

Inside a Broken Clock

Cinéma Vérité

I fell in love with this book on the first page. Sam Rasnake's poems — often metrical, or visually arrayed like a piece of art — are beautifully crafted. In them, we relive great films we have seen, learn how to pitch to a producer, encounter a script in development, and are shown close-up portraits of the directors. Delightful, fresh, full of *superbly* smart, insightful observations about film's ability to model the twinned Janus-faces of comedy and tragedy. Roger Ebert would give *Cinéma Vérité* four stars. So do I.

— Kelly Cherry, winner of the Hanes Poetry Prize, a Pushcart, and three PEN/Syndicated Fiction awards, and author of *The Life and Death of Poetry: Poems*

"Language," the immortal Sergei Eisenstein wrote, "is much closer to film than painting is." And while other poets have explored the entwined connections of film and poetry, no American poet is doing so more effectively today than Sam Rasnake. He writes: *Like the puppeteer's hands/ that refuse to hide or the stir/ of wings... something/ lets go its darker elegance.* But the elusive *other* in these poems never goes away; not at all. What is seemingly lost to the speaker of this and so many other poems in this book appears luminously on every page, as if projected by the magic lanterns of old — framed, examined — with each image fully realized. There is not an outtake, not a single process-shot among the poems in *Cinéma Vérité*. This is the real stuff; the long-rumored master reel — language from the very heart of things.

— Greg Rappleye, author of *A Path Between Houses*, winner of the Brittingham Prize, and *Figured Dark*, winner of the University of Arkansas Press Poetry Series

Cinéma Vérité

poems / sketches / parables

Sam Rasnake

© A-Minor Press
http://aminorpress.com/

Acknowledgements

My thanks to the editors of the following publications in which these poems, sometimes in earlier versions, first appeared:

52/250, Adirondack Review, A-Minor, A Baker's Dozen, Big Muddy, BOXCAR Poetry Review, Connotation Press, Corium Magazine, The Drunken Boat, Emprise Review, fourpaperletters, FRiGG, From East to West, fwriction : review, Midwest Coast Review, MiPOesias, muse apprentice guild, New World Writing (formerly New Mississippi Review), OCHO, Octavo, Otoliths, Poets/Artists, Press 1, Ramshackle Review, Shampoo, The Smoking Poet, Thrush Poetry Journal, UCity Review, and *Wild Goose Poetry Review*

Anthologies: **Best of the Web 2009**: "Chamber Music"; **BOXCAR Poetry Review Anthology 2**: "This is not my testament"; **Deep River Apartments**: "An Ear," originally published as "A Fable"; **MiPOesias Companion 2012**: "Lines Written Under the Influence"; **Flash Fiction Fridays**: "The Wolf Who Cried Boy"; *Whale Sound*: "Chamber Music" and "Michael Powell's Women"

Pushcart nominations: "Cinéma Vérité" by *Ramshackle Review*; "The Dead" by *From East to West*. "Lines Written Under the Influence" was originally published as a broadside by *MiPOesias*.

Cover Design: Eryk Wenziak

Cinéma Vérité is part 3 of the poetry series **Tales of Brave Ulysses**.

Copyright ©2013 by Sam Rasnake

ISBN: 978-0615856957
First Edition, A-Minor Press

– for essentials, special thanks to Felicia Mitchell, Edison Jennings, James Owens, Michelle Elvy, Meg Pokrass, Bill Yarrow, Joani Reese, Gary Hardaway, and Carol Reid

– for Mary, always

– in memory of my father, J. Samuel Rasnake
...independent as a hog on ice...

Contents

I The Way the Story Begins

Lines Written Under the Influence	15
After Kubrick	16
Chamber Music	17
Games of Persuasion	20
A Geometry of Extremes	21
Cravings of the Business	22
Michael Powell's Women	23
Cinéma Vérité	24
Jean-Luc Godard's Love Letter...	25
Disparate Analogues, Three Fables	26
Eine Symphonie des Grauens, in Close-up Study	29
Frame Line	30
Poem to Read Aloud...	31
Among the Wreckage	33
Little by Little, the Beautiful World	36

II Spaces between the Words

Warm Saké with Plucked Samisen...	39
Four Colors	40
Notes on the Cinematographer	44
Lost Connections, Hidden Intentions	45
Omen. Seduction. Reunion.	46
Two-Reeler	47
Woman in Tableaux	49
Dark Fountain	52
False Windows	53
Of *Koyaanisqatsi*	54
MacGuffin	55
You Broke My Heart	56
Everything in Motion	57

Lost Elegy for Hank Quinlan   58
"Something to do with death"   59

III   A Scribbling on the Walls

Right Hand, Left Hand   63
Anything Goes   64
The Wolf Who Cried Boy   65
Aguirre Erect, Alone, a Raft Drifting...   66
A Scribbling on the Walls   67
Third Draft, Suicide Note, Found...   68
All Art Is Betrayal   69
Variation on a Variation of a Mode   70
Begin the Beguine   72
Dinner with Wong Kar-Wai   75
"Which side are you on..."   76
At the Grave of Yasujiro Ozu   77
The Dead   79
After The Falling Man   80
Beggars' Banquet   81
This is not my testament: 82

Chaos will prevail.
   — ***Hiroshima mon amour*** (1959)
   Alain Resnais, Dir.

It's a hard world for little things.
   — ***The Night of the Hunter*** (1955)
   Charles Laughton, Dir.

I

The Way the Story Begins

Lines Written Under the Influence

— Ry Cooder's soundtrack, **Paris, Texas**

The beginning middle and end don't fit
our lives anymore. The shadows are real.
Too much road, I think. Everywhere,
too much away from and nothing toward.
Signs and buildings and plate glass neon.
You don't act the words. Just say them —
The rhythm of bone and soup and wind,
a hawk landing on rocks, newspaper
along asphalt, the whistle of fence line
and railroad tracks to divide the waking
from the dream and a seamless blue
over desert high country. This is
the solitude of happy. The right car
and music, the highway. No borders.

After Kubrick

the world is more
compacted, less

a ball. We don't
talk as much and

the streets are still,
unhammered

piano strings
in a closed

cherry cabinet,
well past midnight,

but in the end,
we kill ourselves

with music and
are glad of it.

Chamber Music

> — after viewing Ingmar Bergman's film trilogy

I. *Through a Glass Darkly*

Is it foolish
to think God
a spider?

a spun moment,
perfect in its
architecture of waiting?
in its raw edge of abandon?

The gull cries
a sudden emptiness
of sea lapping stone.

Wind in heavy grass —
Is that what I carry?

What I carry, I forgive,
what I forgive, I touch
or name or pity

like the fields
soaked with rain,
like voices inside
my mouth, like a love
with no bowl
for keeping.

2. *Winter Light*

Your body, like river-rush
in late November,
craves the early summer.

Our eyes refuse us nothing.

The fence and sky,
tough wings of darkness
expect a storm,
will not be moved.

Sheets thrown back.
The hard gossip we surrender to,
coughed hallelujahs, and guilt
to feed us.

Through a closed window at dusk,
I watch wind jar the hazel tree
by the porch, but hear nothing.

3. *The Silence*

I've no idea where I am.
There's no one to call,
and if there were,
I'd have nothing to tell.

War rumbles through the city
and on the rails.
All the faces are the same.
They speak in tongues, they wear fear
on their shoulders.

There's no one —
But you know this already.

The body I touch is no longer mine.

I spend my time changing words —
translation in a cloud of smoke.
The piano is Bach, *Goldberg Variations*.

This hotel, with its hint of plush,
massive, severe, is mostly empty.
In the corridor, a passing troupe of dwarfs,
the last one in death mask,
is my pretense for loneliness.

Under my window, a scrawny horse
whose ribs could spell my name
pulls at a wagon, loaded with junk
to sell, over the narrow, dirty street,
from one lost intent to the next.

Games of Persuasion

> *– in the gardens at Frederiksbad*

This is the way the story begins.
Just repeated lines. Words shifting
as if place were only stand in for

hand to shoulder or finger to mouth.
Chandeliers to cards to shrub to sky –
this could be anywhere. Don't waste

your time with narrative. A broken shoe,
the long stair, an ache in the unheard wind.
The door always ajar. This is the way

the story begins. In a crowded room.
All those mouths moving, their tongues
a wash of reason – resist, submit,

resist, submit – convincing the world
of mirrors, of broken glass. And what is
laughter any way?   The eye gives

its passion, the breast its lost dream,
the body its fever of want. So, this is
how it begins. In lost letters, photographs,

games of chance. The fear is you might
remember something deep and awful,
something so perfect you wouldn't dare

breathe to anyone. And so you listen –
the sound of feet on gravel, crossing
a garden, has become your waking life.

– L'année dernière à Marienbad (1961), Alain Resnais, dir.

A Geometry of Extremes

> *It's human to lie.*
> *– from **Rashomon** by Akira Kurosawa*

In a dark forest tangle,
in a breath of sun,
three whispers of wind

along the road. What if
I say it rained that day,
what if heat were snow, and

the one thing to remember
is a cloud – how it curved
downward against blue. If

we see it, it must be true then.
Tree, pond, blade. Everything,
little by little, making sense.

Everything, real. The loudest
no means yes, and the dead
speak only of pride, sweat

on the chin, eyes closing
to surrender – reminders
that once lost, lost forever.

In a tangle, in a breath.
A desperate rage of power,
of lust or fear that wills

the body on. The unsayable
your feet, your hands
never dreamed to know.

Leave your mark. Burn
a shadow toward the future
for determined jaws to ponder.

Cravings of the Business

The telephone. A bowl of oranges.
Time to know each other.
Lots of gin. And "Smoke
gets in your eyes" —
Our cravings straddle us,
so I give up humility.
Pleasure is more essential
than fidelity.

Over a white sea of deep shag,
at the far end of the room,
two mannequins are nude, wigless,
in bed, coupling their tessellations
of the body. What we lack
in knowledge, we make up
in silence.

A third, the voyeur,
finds her own remedy.
Everything is madness,
and our needs devour us,
swelling the head with terror,
with demands of possession,
but don't dare listen to me.
I'm only impersonating
a human being.

> – *Die bitteren Tränen der Petra von Kant* (1972),
> R.W. Fassbinder, dir.

Michael Powell's Women

Give me the exotic on-her-own-can-do-
anything kind, cold rain on her face,
in from the hunt, her hounds on a leash.

Holding the deepest secret in the well
of her eyes, she carries over the shoulder
a sack of silence, and tilts to the wind

when she walks. A woman transformed,
trans-mobile, transfixed on *her* moment,
never praying when she needs to, always

running the circles of the vortex she calls risk —
a bit desperate, a bit immortal, but all body
in search of the one body that fits — the place,

the sound, the dream of the whole.
Give me a woman of the mountains,
her bright hair tucked under her habit,

or one bristling at all the burning possibilities
of surrender to the dark perfumes of the world.
A bold wanderer of long grass and deep soil,

afraid of nothing. A woman in motion, whirling
across an empty stage — such sweet dilemmas
as art vs. love — afraid of losing everything.

A woman certain of all the missing parts,
one wrapped in the rage of her want,
another in a reckless sea of paint —

In the scratch of brush over canvas,
in a fall from the sky,
in the raised lens of my camera.

Cinéma Vérité

– for Jeanne Dielman

Each day a habit of things – the do and don't of
alarm to coffee to polished shoes – first breakfast,
then school, then pajamas tucked under the pillow
for days, for months, for years. The bed is folded
away to couch, and the shopping is done. Lost
buttons, empty streets. Even the name disappears.
The mail, elevator, the hall. Mail, elevator, hall.
Lights off, lights on, room to room, for pantry,
for music, knitting, Baudelaire. Clean forks
and spoons, cracked eggs and flour. The hands.
What could possibly be more dull, more empty,
than peeling potatoes with mindless precision
as if it were the reason to breathe, as if it were
some long and steady ache for carving out
the eyes – for washing, for cutting into halves,
then quarters – the water boiling on the stove,
a constant gurgle of steam against tile as the only
comfort while the bastard city offers its trade
in body against body, making whores of us all.

– Jeanne Dielman, 23 Quai du Commerce, 1080 Bruxelles (1975),
    Chantal Akerman, dir.

Jean-Luc Godard's Love Letter to His Wife

A camera tracks slowly the walk over gravel
in rhythm to credits spoken, not written, then
turns its eye as if to say you are here in tangles
of word and desire. A fix of thrill and loss.

Bodies filtered red, white, then blue over voices
flattened by what is unsaid between ankle, thigh,
and chin. The heroes are dead. Empty rooms
with walls washed of color. A tender smile,
a face, tragic and full of flowers, bed, and phone.
Erotic frescoes in a book under swirls of cigarette
smoke. Fights over nothing at all – pasta, green
beans, the slap. These dulled motions of the day.
A toilet as throne, reading in the bath, combing
the wig, putting on socks. The lamp, on and off.
Lost years in hard lines. No touch allowed.

With fires to speak but no will to say, you watch –
steep jags of rocky shoreline, down into the soft
grey of the sea. *Take care*, she writes. Silence.

    – ***Le Mépris*** (1963), Jean-Luc Godard, dir.

Disparate Analogues, Three Fables

– after films by David Lynch

I. An Ear

There couldn't possibly be
anything more lonely than
a single ear lost in a field,
unable to translate the ants
marching through, tough
and ordinary, not able
to hear the wind in weeds
under soft stars, no screams
of desire from the dark
throttle of bodies, no hard
breathing, names melted
into names, no way to be
reattached to the one
story that makes sense.

2. A Face

It's the story of a face – the hunger
of lips for something dark, something
wild, for the smoothed dream of a hard
truth that rides the winding hills' slow
night above the valley's soft shimmer
of dots – red and white – moving,
holding place. It's the tremble
of bushes and trees – another story
on its arc. *Every story has its way,*
David Lynch, both hands undulating
the air as he speaks. And it is true.
A line of song, a thread of smoke,
the narrative you've always believed
but could never quite make clear.

3. The Mouth and Tongue

"So, you have a new role
to play, I hear?" No way
of being anything but true,
and no way of knowing *is,
was,* or *will be* – troubled
in the blisters of the day
to day. It's strange what
love does to the mouth
and tongue. A quivering
dance of thighs. Light slips
fisheyed over pink walls
and carpet, swallows their
bodies whole. It must have
something to do with time.

Eine Symphonie des Grauens, in Close-up Study

*I had read Bram Stoker's Dracula, and I had seen those images before —
but not out in the open, outside of my head projected against a wall for
everyone to share.*
    — Klaus Koblitz, after viewing **Nosferatu** *the first time,
       from the novel* **Kino***, by Jürgen Fauth*

Still, the music plays though no one listens under the screen's
great flicker — too taken, too caught up with the shock. Nothing
could prepare — not the cellos' deep groan at the bottom of bowing
violins moving in wave from the pit as if the world depended on
that rhythm for its turning, not the rumble of tympani giving order
to darkness, and not the seats' tense shuffle of legs and feet.
Nothing could avert the look.

                                    Always the eyes. After the beating
of horses' hooves crossing the mountain pass, a hush troubles
the sounding clock and cut thumb from the table's midnight meal.
Eyes just visible over wrinkled papers — such a strange,
lugubrious script.

                We wait the creaking of an opened door — for
death itself under the archway, arms stretched tight beside the hips,
long fingers fanning out for some malevolent, unspeakable craving
— first oboe, then strings — for delirious surrenders of the body
to the will.

                Shadows creep the tilted wall, banister, and bed —
both hands reaching, that rodent grin with its burning. He rises
from the silent wood, climbs the ship's hold with its wet smells
of turned earth, then walks the murky prow below block
and spar. Rope dangles from the deck. All fragments
of obsession and need to do the self in — while
wisps of smoke feather the moon's
unbendable story to opiate fogs
of a stunned perfection.

Frame Line: "A New World of Gods and Monsters"

– quotation from James Whale's **Bride of Frankenstein**

Long after *The Invisible Man*
and *The Old Dark House*,
after hot Sunday
brunches, and stroke,

an electrical storm inside
his brain every time
he closed his eyes –
a throb no doctor's pill

could numb – would not
still his thoughts to bodies
tangled in barbed wire,
to slender youth

on a cutting room floor,
life among the surreal
graves – would not stop
his phantom smells

of death or beef
drippings, until he,
up to his eyeballs
in living, found

the silent waters
of his pool deeper than
he'd ever imagined
possible

Poem to Read Aloud While Positioning a Framed Sketch of Frankenstein's Monster on a Table

Late-night ramblings — rants from underground — appear to imply that words, if spelled correctly, are dead, or at best, meaningless — wounded, mortally. If you could hear their silences after the still-point of their glottal ravings into the air that no one hears, you would agree. Their dialect is on the lam, hiding while search lights sweep a black, empty sky.

Ice has melted in my glass. Yes.

All I know could be written in one sentence — maybe add an ellipsis for good measure.

The Brownsville tape is water damaged.

A History of Western Philosophy, volume IV, is missing, and I suspect foul play. A philosopher thief — Who would have thought?

What I have to say about modern music could find itself lost on the head of a pin. What I have to say about the head of a pin should not be heard by children. What I've learned of children, I've forgotten. What I've forgotten...

Sylvia Plath is dead. Paul Celan, dead. Jesus, dead. David Cronenberg is alive, I think. He breaks the pattern. What does that mean? What does he mean, rethinking William S. Burroughs? What does he know about Blondie that I don't know. And spider webs? What can I say?

* I'm not who I say I am. *But you haven't said. * *Then what you've heard is true.* *

What I write is false.

Franz Kafka is not dead. I spoke to him on the phone. He was a bit surprised, I'm sure. Said he couldn't speak long. Had to go for smokes. Such is greatness.

These words have nothing to say. These words refuse to leave, refuse to be carried off. They stay. They listen for a comrade, listen for an opening. In the morning they will have all been turned to beetles, on their backs, legs in the air, unsure of any present they can breathe into. And from their beds, worst of all, when the paragraph is done, they'll remember nothing.

Well, then, everything is stolen isn't it. [And this is where I'm speaking directly to you... * *Write it!* *Elizabeth would say, if she were here.]

So, if this came to you in tomorrow's mail — say, a chain for luck — would you send it to three of your closest friends?

[Note to the reader: Portions of the work set aside with an * should be read aloud four times, then precipitously forgotten. The writer will remind you, on a need-to-know basis, when those words may, in fact, save your soul.]

Among the Wreckage

– after viewing Roberto Rossellini's War Trilogy

I. Rome

– for Marcello Magnani

The perfect image of war should be the boy
in white cassock, rushing to his mother,
the only religion he understands – she's
dead in the street, gunned down as she ran
– and in a blind rage of fear and loss

he tries to shake her body to life, but it will
not do, he's only boy and she the world,
so he kicks the air, the priest, any uniform
who would stop him, anyone who would
say that spring will come again

– 1943

2. Naples

– for Pasquale

All language obscures
until it's impossible to

know old from new –
friend, enemy, self,

other. Three years of
allied bombing, 20,000

civilians dead, and the city,
nothing more than heaps

of waste, brick, and cans –
a cold maze of grottos,

a blister of fragments
in a war for shoes.

– 1944

3. Berlin

    – for Edmund Koehler

The dust is everything. All times between living and the dead blur to nothing, to one foot in front of the other, to a slice of raw potato, and water that hints at tea.

You should see this place. Dark hallways with wrecked doors, empty stairwells where music is silence. A broken city – Piles of rubble here and here and here. So many.

    – 1947

Little by Little, the Beautiful World

– the state library, Berlin

People that do come here are the sort that have something lost, a hole to fill. They never miss. I watch them. On Saturdays a huddle of kids and story time. The furious and determined note-taker, sketching dunes and rocky wastes as though only she could find the beauty in such a place. The one who comes every Thursday to write and write in a small notebook. Never seems to finish. The old man and his war crimes. His thrown chair in a vacant lot, the only comfort, or is it guilt for surviving. The woman who sits by the stairs on Tuesdays but never reads anything. I wonder what she waits for. And the talkers by the magazine rack with their great tales. The checkout desk. The unused elevator. Such a lonely place when empty. All those books, and no eyes to connect with. I clear my throat, scrape my chair over tile, closer to the table, drop my shoulders, turn the page.

*– **Der Himmel über Berlin*** (1987), Wim Wenders, dir.

II

Spaces between the Words

**Warm Saké with Plucked Samisen,
a Tray of Food, a Tangle of Bodies**

— Ogu, Tokyo, 1936

This is the moment that's never enough,
that you will spend your life trying to
get back to, the moment of abandon,

of forcing an exquisite thread of universe
through a tiny hole. There's a certain
beauty in what we lose. Every yes,

every no is perfect chance, perfect surrender.
His eyes hold everything. Her fingers gather
the stilted world, rumbling under the balls

of their feet, into something livable.
This is before the war, before
the world shifts off center, when

the machine rules absolutely —
unbalanced and unwilling.
These are givens. After the man dies,

the woman cuts off his penis and scrotum,
carries them, like small children,
hotel to hotel, until she is found, finally.

There's no hate, no anger, just a hunger
to feed. No one wants to punish her
for her heart, for the meaning that slips away

when the last rattle of air escapes.

*— **Ai no korída** (1976), Nagisa Ôshima, dir.*

Four Colors

— after four films by Krzysztof Kieślowski

Gold

It's a river of dead leaves
in the cold of turning fables —
where a cup of steaming tea,
its bag in a swirl, waits.

The whole notes are sung,
the world inverted,
and the love is made.

Like the puppeteer's hands
that refuse to hide or the stir
of wings, something disappears
from me today, something
lets go its darker elegance
for the insurgent grace
of a determined heart.

Blue

The sugar cube is soaked
with coffee before it's plopped.
You could use a long, steady cry,
but the mice in your rooms are too loud,
the voices along the stair, too intimate,
and those who love you — if
that is even the word — too lost
in the refraction of miserable silences.

It's the music that haunts,
the missing lines of ink on paper,
the flute with no streets to fill.
A stone wall on which the hand bleeds
beneath a numbed and empty heaven
with its long hollows of disconnection.

White

And only this remains when the living burns away leaving pigeon shit on the shoulder as a reminder that humiliation is the essential purpose of flight not discovery not forgiveness and certainly not a love that will not have its way or find solution for its dilemma for that hunger for the other to defer capitulate succumb to hold on so when the story begins there is black then sound and only then an image

Red

This is a poem about what is heard, not what is seen
A poem about pity, about an ache for such a loss
Lines for risk, for luck, for wager, for cherry cherry cherry
        for the one gift a coin should bring
        for random pages in a book
        the dusky strings of Van Den Budenmayer
        a stumbled walk across an unlikely stage
        for unreal, pretend, ersatz
The reader must never forget: it's a life made up of many lives
        a fraternal order of should have been
These lines are against indifference, are lines to make you commit
Lines to make you angry, to make you cry
If asked if you have loved, you will answer – no
If asked about grief – *and say it with me* : no
        an immaculate no
The connections are broken, the window, broken, the battery, dead
There's no laughter here, but there will be smiles
     can't you feel it, even now, tugging at your mouth
A smirk *perhaps*
An epiphany *to be sure*
Or breath of life, or second chance
Someone should have told you

Notes on the Cinematographer

        Words push against
        other words to say
        what is most needed

        And here I write
what is found is irrelevant
what is hidden is your life
    the desire to destroy
    the erotic the spiritual
    the singular moment

    Flatten the moment
      Write nothing
     Let the silence
      be everything

The nightingale is loved
for its song and its song
  is always the same
  The donkey breathes
  and we are changed
The sheep bell reminds us
  of the need to be lost
And the piano finds
perfection in the space
  between each note

— ***Au hasard Balthazar*** (1966), Robert Bresson, dir.

Lost Connections, Hidden Intentions

The geometry of bodies in motion —
an earlobe, eyes intent on an unknown,
a face turning — is the calculation of loss.
Breathing swells both chests to one.
Hands in a desperate search for what's missing
would like to touch but never do.

In an overstuffed summer room, a rotating
fan gives voice to love's impossibilities —
between beautifully frail and inevitable ruin.
Nothing connects. Forget the mushroom cloud
of a building, the car with corpse being pulled
from a river, the scream of money.

Lamp, books, and curtain. An ashtray
displaced, a couch too small for coupling,
or the phone's busy signal. None of these stay.
A wind among trees and stacks of tile
with scaffolding. An empty street in shadow.
Water runs from barrel to storm drain.

One streetlight, in a frenzied burn of dusk to darkness,
leaves such a blinding, present absence
for the uncertain morning to find.

— *L'eclisse* (1962), Michelangelo Antonioni, dir.

Omen. Seduction. Reunion.
— the Poet's Commentary for Mizoguchi's **Ugetsu monogatari**

— for Bill Yarrow

What I love most is the heavy mist on Lake Biwa, drifting, as if
a shore must loom somewhere in the nervous silence between

the distant thuds of war. Everything changes. Realities blur real
with *real*, truth with *truth*. So the story begins: a simple man

of pots and kiln, unsure of his art. His great flaw. The price?
Brother, family, the only life he's known. Abandoned sandals
     Omen
near the temple. Coins of the trade. Shades move over weed and
ruin — entanglements of the mind. The dance to forbidden song,

the giving in to bath and silks. Things are not what they seem.
Stone garden to field & tree & food — two lovers in an obsession

of wills and time. Sanskrit written on the body for protection,
for clarity. Then the waking. Maybe it's a story about beauty,
     Seduction
about knowing the self, the moving on, no matter the loss.
He walks for days, the deep fevers of the road still burning,

though shame is now his gift and the need to make amends.
Then he's back home, circling through the dark, empty house.

There's nothing. No one. But when he comes round again,
in one long take, there she is — the dead woman, the love he left —
     Reunion
cooking a stew over the fire that was ash just moments before.
The child is sleeping. It's a story of betrayal, of forgiveness,

of words left unsaid. He eats, he drinks, he sleeps. She works
thread into a kimono. This is her art. Morning will find her

gone. No way to explain this, and grief doesn't care why.
One day follows the next. And so on. He'll make his pots.

Two-Reeler

fade in:
The car always breaks down outside
a small town with no name.

quick cuts:
Thick stands of trees on
both sides of the asphalt,
potholes waiting to be
filled in with a spring thaw.

collage:
One gas station, three trucks, two cars, quarts of oil stacked
in the window, a gaggle of old men — gnarled hats and ratty
coats — nothing better to do, by the candy machine,
drinking orange sodas, their talk a bit garbled —

voice over:

"The baby could look like anybody"
"John or Joey, Mike or Dave"
"That plant's played out"
"In everybody's business"
"She shot her, who shot him —"

— having to do with
the one black sheep the town claims, who lives down
the road a piece, her unlit windows the subject
of all whispers —

                                        soundtrack:
                                        My days, they are
quick cuts: *the highway kind*
Large pile of stones,   *they only come to leave*
a broken mailbox,
dark clouds over
railroad tracks,

              soundtrack:
Footsteps on gravel then stone walk then porch.
A hand knocks at the door, and it opens.

                                chocolate Lab running,
boy and rake in a swirl of leaves,
a cold rain just starting.

fade out:

Woman in Tableaux

[middle]: My Life, chapter 3

— ***Vivre sa vie***, *Jean-Luc Godard*

A street, thick-shadowed and mostly empty, with record shop, apartment, café, theater, is no real match for innocence. What she sees on the screen burns to the bone — Jeanne d'Arc in a fit of perfection or grief, not able to bend, not willing to stop, can't help but question everything she touches, everything she wants — body and soul, body and soul. She gives herself only to herself, and finds that deliverance sometimes is no deliverance at all. You may believe in lines, but there aren't any. Truth is nothing more than spirals of beauty and lust, essence and moment. Running like mad over the stiff mechanics of all things opposite, she lives simply because she says she lives, her words finding her at last — or should I say "at beginning" — finding her where she has always been.

[end]: My Say

– ***An Angel at My Table***, Jane Campion

In the ship's long wake – in back of eight slow years of crowded wards with electrodes, in a role, in a willing trap for empty pages to fill – in the hush of wind and sea from Auckland to London to pain, there's no pity, no sentimental hogwash. It's the body you ache to know, the *you* you will the self to find – from first words to something real.

There was a missing, surely – a dark hole, something to want.

Sheep still graze the wet, steep hills, a world that never stopped its beautiful plundering.

Always a third person, a *they* or a *she* – you breathe in the wild, finally, and the thinnest line of happy finds the corners of your mouth. You type away into the unmoving darkness – an *I*, a *me*.

[beginning]: A Restless Moment

— ***Fa yeung nin wa***, Wong Kar-Wai

Mirrors never lie. Plucked rhythms underneath the voiced violin whisper and whisper their missed chances to the rain.

She's always stepping out — up and down stairs, along the street, a noodle thermos swaying in her hand, thin wisps of smoke, those slow, delicious walks she can't resist, the narrow hall awash in red — a shoulder, a touch, unspoken words.

I wonder how it all began, she says, those lush nights of betrayal, all the hidden spaces for handbag and tie, and how we came to know. We won't be like them — we love to eat — that's what we do, that's *all* we do.

The opened window ripples a hot curtain — in the room tucked away for writing, for the story never written, for the eyes, glancing away a last time to find some meaning, some purpose, lost in silence.

Dark Fountain

    *— after Jacques Rivette's **La Belle Noiseuse***

He'd let go ten years before.
Now, his charcoal stick scrapes
canvas — a line, a curve, soft

hollows of back and hip and
thigh. She stands, center room,
in the perfect moment inside

his head that will never find
its finished form, never give
itself away as though starved

or mad. His hand will ache
with its hours, his eye will
search for what it cannot see.

False Windows

> *Are you afraid?... of yourself?... of me?*
> *— from **Ma Nuit chez Maud** by Eric Rohmer*

Outside the snow is like the one falling
on Clermont-Ferrand that Christmas when
Rohmer had waited years for the moment
of storm that made talk inevitable, and could not
be missed, or another year would have to come
round for the setting to work. His art was such
a force, he commanded even the elements as prop,
as character, as silence for story — an ordinary day
given to Pascal, religious chant and choice, infidelities
into the late hours — two bodies, one room, one bed —
when talk is never just talk — feeble declarations of
a false and hidden life where desire is willed to its knees,
finally — which is what it had wanted all along —
there in the warm, cozy spaces between the words.

Of *Koyaanisqatsi*

Godfrey Reggio says, "We no longer have the words to explain the world we live in." They can never tell us what is – in fact, words tell us nothing. Deep layers of cloud, roiling in their own perfection, we say, and over the sea's great curls of time, mountains, always the sky's careful, most stunning lover. But the talk misleads, misdirects. Mistaken lives and purposes – that's our métier, and we're proud of it. Urban sprawl is our grand illusion. Our geographies of madness, swarms of faces, floods of red, of white streaming north & south, the growl and burn of the gross national product, east & west. We breathe, push buttons, drive on. *Our unholy wires*, we pray, *keep us connected. Cut open the ground, stop all rivers so we can live in the unlivable. Lead us by ghosts of steel and concrete in such tight, merciless rows for blocks, for miles, and time zones. Surely stone will become a handful of dust. Amen.* We grow fat in our silk beds. We propagate in our own juices. We die.

MacGuffin

I'm afraid I've been guilty of leading you down the garden path – or should it be up? I never can remember.
                                    *– **The 39 Steps***

Here, in the land of the somewhat dead are all
the answers you could ever wish for. A dream,
a breath in whisper, the wet hillside under heavy

skies that go on forever or seem to. And then
there's the well with its coins polished by cold
and time that scatter the bottom – their own stories,

each one a gift from an uneasy hand, from fingers
too wrenched with letting go. And by the way,
isn't it remarkable how a little sex sells – just

the thought of what could be might be enough –
eyes over the fence, behind the curtain, across
a table, the long room waiting. But back to threads

of narrative: *he*, obviously mistaken for someone,
for something he's not, and *she*, unwilling or thought
to be a perfect cool to the moment, always find

a truth, but it's in what they could make, and not
what they do make – Nothing could be less plausible,
but here it is again and again – we know it by

heart. In fact, we are its heart – *thump thump,
thump thump.* Someone's at the door, of course,
or it's the phone, an e-mail that finds you – and

we wake up. A new morning, new winter of disbelief
made unforgettable by ice and rain on a day when you
only ache for covers, for darkness, for comfy clothes,

for what's missing, for what must always be so.

You Broke My Heart

This is this. – to John Cazale (1935-1978)

To find the character, find the pain –
There's the mantra – eh, John?
                                      Nothing
expected. Not the raised eyebrows,
glancing away, then checking your fly.
A wheel of smoke, a jester's bag, but
everything the right fit.
                              Both hands
the constant pun, your long hair's
receding line, no mistake and no
forgetting.
                   Veins in the forehead
thick with waiting. Hard corners of
this perfect jaw make the moment
an easy dark to step into.
                            No one sees
you spitting up blood.
                        Every breath
a question, every word tongued a rock,
razor-edged, in the belly – to cut
its way out – leaving as reflection,
such a solitary scrap,
in the car window.
                      "Beautiful," you say.

Everything in Motion

— Texas panhandle, 1917

In the middle of a great field
a house, Victorian ornate, so empty
no other voice could hope to find
its detailed walls with photographs —
not family exactly, but the desperate
need to hold one, to make something
of such an unforgiving place — that
stare out its tall windows and long porch.

Words are useless. Wind in the wheat.
Mist on the pond. Geese crossing
a thick sky. The lives we find are fire
and locust. Scarecrow in silhouette
against purple. Dull thunder of steam
tractor, hard hands, and bent backs.

The end bullies its way into our joints,
moves us closer until the face we see
we no longer recognize. Railroad tracks
disappear into a cold, wooded darkness,
leaving their silence only to fill
this timeless warp of finished days.

*— **Days of Heaven** (1978), Terrence Malick, dir.*

Lost Elegy for Hank Quinlan

– Los Robles, 1957

What does it matter what you say when truth
is not an option, when your future's all
used up in shadows over empty walls,
in whispers you should never hear but can't
stop listening, a ticking in your head
as if dreams were ever enough, as if
one word or even two could be the sum
of tarot cards in smoky rooms, music
from the pianola so old it's new,
the lost beauty with its bent for grieving,
a place to hide, an almost life – the touch
for grace and obsession, for sorry luck,
the hard nights drifting on dirty water
– clean and silent – all measured for a fall.

– ***Touch of Evil*** (1958), Orson Welles, dir.

"Something to do with death"

— Sweetwater Station, Arizona, 1869

Red dust from Monument Valley through
swinging doors in Spain, miracles of time
and space among the worn buttes and olive

ground. That breath of myth we never escape —
a well, a bath, a gandy's cup. The town begins
in the desert by spike, by rail, by land cut,

somewhere between madness and providence,
with leftover timber from Orson Welles' take
on Falstaff — his best film according to some.

Well-honed battles and blood crossing the sea
into Arizona's geography of lost innocence,
with deafening cracks of gunfire, eyes in extreme

close-up, the body of a woman's perfect resolve.
The face as landscape that needs no word.
Flapping dusters, an old windmill screeching,

one fly buzzing, water dripping to a hat's brim.
Everything expendable. Everyone. An unbearable
wait for the train's scream of steel on steel.

Nothing is as it seems. Greed, vengeance, hope.
Discordant rattles, *duello finale*, all sweat and swoon.
A man rides away. A woman brings water.

*— **Once Upon a Time in the West** (1968), Sergio Leone, dir.*

III

A Scribbling on the Walls

Right Hand, Left Hand

– Spike Lee, Summer 1989

The life you build with your hands – all sweat & rage & music too loud – isn't a life after all. It's only color, and everything it's not. On the hottest day of the year, squeezed tight against the thinnest of walls, the demanding street reminds you that no one is going anywhere, that truth is its own dark math, that no dream is the only dream. Words mean nothing. Children with their babies, old men waiting, Korean market, pizzeria, lines drawn in concrete, and heads too hard, too thick to move. From her window seat Mother Sister, such a tough, forgiving soul, watches the long and steady spiral-down of power and smart, holding her eyes to the sun with her wish for rain.

Anything Goes

— William S. Burroughs, Tangier, 1959

Leading an ordinary life
was never the plan:

>   easy to lose your way
>   in clouds of tea smoke,
>   in delicious elixirs
>   of herb & bark, mixed
>   in alabaster bowls,
>   that traffic the street —

>   easy to uncover
>   the secrets of humiliation,
>   to catch the silent *yes* —

>   the air, perfumed with it.

———————

Hands spread on the ground anatomical charts for particular spells outside cafés where giant aquatic black centipede is the specialty, a perfect remedy for any ailment, where customers — European mostly, or American, glazed with oblivion — wait the slow mutation of man to bug to man.

*— **Naked Lunch** (1991), David Cronenberg, dir.*

The Wolf Who Cried Boy

There was a boy who cried wolf. We know this fable, and call it the beginning of literature. Thing with no name. But truth is — it was a wolf who cried boy. According to Kafka, anticipating Nabokov, the origin of literature is when a wolf comes down from the crags, out of the dark, forbidding forest, and into the open, crying, "Boy! Boy!" but there is no boy. The pack is, of course, astounded, mesmerized. Someone first tells it. Someone writes it down. Dreams it. And so on.

There had to be a wolf, eventually — we all know this — to write it down. A book written by a wolf — about people no less, about trucks, banks, and pots full of water, about blazing fires and mountain laurel, sheep and cattle. On the back cover, he wears a jacket and jeans, a fedora and scarf, one paw at his hip. His bio reads: "His work has been widely published in *The Village Voice*, *Conundrum*, *Teton Tales*, and *Alpha*. The first wolf to be recipient of a Fulbright, he studied literature and architecture in the Carpathians. For two years he wrote a weekly column for the *Denver Times*, 'The Poet and the Beast.' Living in the Wyoming Basin, he directs a creative writing program from his den."

The story begins... *There were no pigs' huts of straw or stick or stone. No chimney or door. Nothing worth his time to enter, nothing to tear down for another meal — which was quite disturbing, even for a wolf, since the times were so depressed and one never knew where the next meal, or if and when — might be coming.* Of the book, critics write of how well the protagonist assimilates the mind of a pig. Thumbs up. Five stars. Book of the Week. A sales ranking of 383. "More real than real."

— ***Nabokov on Kafka*** (1989), Peter Medak, dir.

Aguirre Erect, Alone, a Raft Drifting, Overrun with Monkeys, 1561

Chickens, pigs and statuary of the Virgin —
stupid nobility — conquistadors dragging cannons
over the Andes and slaves shouldering women
in sedan-chairs — we descend through clouds.

Forty-nine days and I am standing. I am.
The river, between bush silence, fevers its way to sea —
But then, weakness deserves abandonment.
Ursúa hanged, left for cannibals. His beautiful Inez.
And Guzman, fat puppet, emperor of nothing, fool.

I'll marry Flores, oh child — a dynasty in your bulge.
I've set my teeth on power, gold, fame and chewed the world.
The taste was wonderful, a continent on my tongue.

We will endure.

I'm the Wrath of God. If I tell birds to die,
they drop from the trees.

Who else is with me?

> — ***Aguirre, der Zorn Gottes*** (1972), Werner Herzog, dir.

A Scribbling on the Walls

It's like the dead realizing, finally,
they must be dead too, easing into
their smoothed and whispered oblivion –
a blot of time, twice-lived, below the ruins.

A man obsessed, a woman, an image of a face.
Isn't that how it always begins?

Trust, disappointment, madness –
the scars of more than a lifetime.

What is it you look for on this page,
where is it you wander to? –
in the voice's dark timbre
as you breathe the words aloud,
as you speak the fear into place –

This is a real table. A real couch,
glass cabinet, a fire screen
with its painting of pond and heron –
The bamboo plant and bowl, cups of tea,
the thimble box – They're all real.

The reckoning of a truth is lonely business.

When the body fails, or falls, when the dream
implodes of its own weight, and silence is the story,
the eyes opening is what you will most remember.

> – *La Jetée* (1962), Chris Marker, dir. /
> *Vertigo* (1958), Alfred Hitchcock, dir.

Third Draft, Suicide Note, Found in a Book

— Yukio Mishima to Yukio Mishima, November 1970

Your life is craft, a terrible shadow of words in the knot of sword vs. pen, scratched in blood for all the days turned years of child to man to art — as it was intended, as its truth and perfect purpose drift the hard silence of an empty, miserable world and the modern guise you've learned to hate

Truth always hides in art, you say, in a stroke of the pen, long sweep of the brush, the plucked string, in sad laughter of grief, and the Noh, Kabuki, St. Sebastian, all rites of love and death under a bleeding sun, the sky as cold as the deepest winter in Japan —

The horses have fled, the pavilion, burned, and the woman of pain with her dark razor watches over your sleep, your last day, last moment, last samurai

The quiet, steady motion of the hand, such beauty beyond words, is your art

*— **Mishima: A Life in Four Chapters** (1985),*
   Paul Schrader, dir.

All Art Is Betrayal

Like the hot air balloon with its brief
and staggered flight before falling
to the ground in such a deadly heap.

Horse hooves pounding the river's
smoky shallows, each furtive blast
a world of probability against plague.

Wild geese over the city's rape to ruin
in the silent rage that only distance gives.
Or naked bodies, their torches lit, in a run

through a thick wood of midsummer mist,
while the nightingale's song, much older
than time, unfolds its deepest pleasure.

Vows to silence, then an ache for the real,
for the impenetrable cold that defies the hand,
for the impossible gift of a restless spring.

       — *Andrei Rublev* (1966), Andrei Tarkovsky, dir.

Variation on a Variation of a Mode

I'll begin with Julio Cortázar, "What remains to be said is always a cloud, two clouds, or long hours of a sky perfectly clear," then turn the camera to my own face. He turns the camera, and the strap falls across his left wrist, and snaps the shout. Suddenly, and it was over before I noticed what had happened, the young boy runs out of the park — Paris or London or Memphis — out of the story, and into my poem, my prose poem, a flash even — Borges must be so proud somewhere. If I listen closely, the pen's scraping on the page speaks the words. He has to listen closely, bending his ear to his notebook. The furnace has cut on. It's February though he's not certain of the year, but he's sure it's the year of record snows.

There's a woman in the story — there's always a woman in the story — and it's the same woman, sometimes blond, sometimes brunette, though she's new to me, but her face is familiar, her cheeks sloping marble-like to both exquisite temples, with the softest of ears, and eyes that stop you cold, and lips whispering golden words against your neck, her hand always stretched toward the lens of a Nikon S.

I know the man with his black tongue and dark suit is not far off. He's out of his car now. He's been parked there for some time, maybe reading, maybe watching. I hear his footsteps and decide to add that sound to the piece, and it's a good sound: the *clomp, clomp, clomp* that only thin soles over asphalt can give.

The time is unclear, but it's real, and it's late. He's on a sidewalk — his car, a convertible, must be parked nearby. A sea of faces — He writes "sea" but decides against it — ~~sea~~ — *I'm on the sidewalk now, a _____ of faces moving in synch* — He'll come back to this part later — on a night, a warm one at that. But it's not the park, not the story or poem, or even the club he finds himself wandering into — or is it chasing or being chased, I never can remember — and it doesn't really matter since they're all the same. Instead, it's a film. The Yardbirds' "Stroll On," at first a low rumble, then, as he gets closer — distinct and loud. There's a crowd. Most are standing, one couple dances in the back of the room, and no one is talking.

He rolls with the reel, the hot light of the projector making everything clear and alive over the seats and heads and onto the screen. He's very pleased that he began with clouds and ended with a film in a not-so-crowded theater. I am pleased. That's true, and I don't know why. What's that? —

Alternate ending, 1:
One ends with pigeons or sparrows, one with a mimed game of tennis, and another with a crossed out word. The intent is to go back to the page and write a word that fits, and he will do it. Just not now.

Alternate ending, 2:
He's eating waffles with coffee. A paperback and journal on either side of the plate. One pen, one pencil.

Alternate ending, 3:
It'll never be known how this has to be told is his favorite passage. "I can't do better than that," he says. These are the only words actually spoken.

— "Las Babas del Diablo" (1964), short story, Julio Cortázar /
        Blow-Up (1966), Michelangelo Antonioni, dir.

Begin the Beguine

I've been trying to work on my novel this past month, mostly late at night. Call me Herman. Call me Jeanette. Call me Franz. But the poems keep getting in the way. I have to stop writing the draft to diddle with lines or stanzas. Sometimes a metaphor, an alliteration or two. And for what? Who'll read it anyhow? In print or e-book, e-mail or blog? Does it even matter? A loud thud of a *NO*.

In the meantime my characters are stuck in an ugly motel room, just off Highway 95, trying to decide if they'll head north — And here the plot should focus on why Ann gives up her dream of being a forensic specialist so she can build instruments by hand, just like her Dad. So far, she's built fourteen guitars. All on the run. The authorities keep chasing her. Two units — suits really — have been assigned to her case. But she's always one double-cross ahead of them. They're determined to bring her back to her senses. Kicking or screaming, love it or leave it, living or dead — doesn't matter. As long as she comes back and does what she's supposed to. And everyone will be happy ever after. Sort of. Isn't that what it's about anyway?

Or, the characters are trying to decide if, just after dawn, they should go east instead. Follow a line of geese to the coast. Get a boat. Get a room. Blend in. Do some fishing, a little crabbing, rake some clams. Sit in the sand, early evenings, soundside, just to watch the sun go down on the Pamlico, then build a fire. Taste salt in the wind. Get up early. Do it all again.

They could head west or south, but there's no time for hunting the child that ran away. That would cost me a couple of months in writing time. Or, a wreck on some back road. A medical emergency in the parking lot of a hospital. Robbery at a nuclear power plant. That could bring in a terrorist angle. Good-guy-bad-guy sort of thing. He's forced to do it because "they" have his son, his daughter, his lover. Somebody. She's forced to do it because "they" have "him" or "her" or "both". Wait a minute. I could write in two people forced by a terrorist group to rob a nuclear plant. Only they don't know about each other. Parallel action. The terrorists are just playing for the best odds. The plan could be to sabotage the plant, then have the two, without knowing the other's purpose or identity, kill each other. End of story. Terrorists walk away.

Maybe I could just write all these threads into separate chapters. That could work, maybe even be made into a movie or a TV series. I'd have to tie them together, and that might be too hard. Too much work. I'm just not that good. Or, maybe I'm too good. I could write this in a complex way. Series of novels. Three, four, maybe seven or eight books. We're talking a lot of money and royalties. The high life.

There's a question of titles though. *In the Mood for Killing?* What about *Seven Killers for Seven Brothers* or *Killer and Her Sisters?* One of these could work. Maybe *Two or Three Things I Know about Killing. Pulp Kill.* All possibilities. If you have the right title, the story pours onto the page – just like a river.

The titles for the books could focus on numbers in some way: One Night, Two Cities, Three for Tango, Four Horses... Or the alphabet: A is for All Along the Watchtower... B for Busted, C for Cabriole... and the rest. Or I could use people's names: Ann. Charlie. Pat or Cameron. This could be endless. The names of streets, states, or countries. Something in the something. That might be the angle I'm looking for. The way to start – midstream:

"The letter was in the drawer." —

"The car wasn't in the drive as it should have been. This time." —

"We hear footsteps. Frantic. Someone running. Shadows moving. Someone is following. Lights along the hill, down to the bridge, then a blanket of sparkles as far as we can see." —

"She could be in Portland by now." —

The story will find its own way.

I'll twist the plot a bit: a loaded gun, mistaken identity, or the least likely syndrome.

There's another way, of course. At some point, the writing has to stop. The characters, for all their promise, will stay seated, frozen in the narrative, their eyes gone empty, all talk finished, the room a dark silence, and still. Nothing moving. Dead on the page until a hand lifts it — and this could be yours — turning it over or a finger sliding across the screen —

A porch light turns on. Two cars pass. The wind, almost talking, shakes the boxwoods along the walk, letting you know the night will be a long one. Again.

Dinner with Wong Kar-Wai

Our lives are measured out
on slender threads, impossible
to ignore — in the back alleys,
in front rooms — obsessing all
the numbed routines that tell us
who we are, tell us there must be
some change — We walk, we eat —
a slow pace against thick speed:

Chef salads with Cantonese opera
on late-night television — black coffee
or whiskey, roast pork and rice —
lychees, pineapple, sardines —

The escalator ride gives way
to a steaming bowl of noodles
while the city smears and jerks
closer to an edge of millennium,
closer to the clockwork of when
it's gone, it's gone for good

I go West, you stay put —
each of us full of his own
fierce design for the beautiful,
for the simple made perfect,
for the sky, dark and open

"Which side are you on..."

> — *thoughts to Barbara Kopple while working on* **Harlan County USA**

This is the house, white clapboard
in sore need of a fresh coat with
its red tin roof, in the mountains
near the state line where

the filmmaker works on her movie.
The feather tick bed where she sleeps,
where she stares the ceiling into dream,
into a crawlspace of black

dust a mile underground. The fireplace,
charred brick of a hundred stories
to keep her warm. The front porch
swing, with its creaking,

where she sits at dusk, loses herself
in the wet, darkening trees.
The wind to whisper a path
into thick hollows

while she studies her gifts.
And windows, so cool
to touch, to hold the world
as if it were the truth.

— *Roan Mountain, Tennessee, 1976*

At the Grave of Yasujiro Ozu

His name doesn't appear on the block
of gray stone – only the character *mu*.

Like a stretch of tracks in winter long
after the train has passed. Snow drifting.

Like the silence of people crossing far
hallways. Doors and rooms never seen.

Clothes folded neatly into a worn case
before the trip. An apple peeled, its dark

curl of skin dangling from troubled fingers.
Lines scribbled by a window before dawn.

The Dead

waste time, put their heads down
on desks to dream illogical trips
to laundromats they talk too much
they read

                     paperbacks and cut out pages
from magazines for poster boards
they give blood then have their navels pierced
because they're good citizens

                                  go to the fridge
during the show for cheese and crackers
so they can make it back by commercial break
they do long division and know
the geography of eastern Asia

                            the dead
have telescopes and guitar picks
stack boxes in the closet
they watch all the Hammer films
like Christmas trees and rain
but not on Saturdays
the dead put coffee in the coffee maker
and with the sound muted they read
the scrolling news at the bottom of the screen

they know the scientific names for plants
don't notice the weather
are too distracted by trains
use prophylactics

                      claim to understand
modern art
know the body is a temple

                        they document
all sources
            understand their cups of tea
they cry miserable tears
never offend

            and refuse
to write anything
that is not silver or true or given

        Silence goes faster backwards.
            *– from **Orphée** (1950),* Jean Cocteau, dir.

After The Falling Man

A lonely ten
seconds very
public in its
impossibility
to see to get at
to tell a grace
a perfect stillness
turned on its head
no one wants but
we look anyway
can't say can't see
can't talk about
still falling still
falling we want
our cake and
beauty too

— *9/11: The Falling Man* (2006), Henry Singer, dir.

Beggars' Banquet

*For the Lord God omnipotent reigneth
forever*, or at least until we find a home.
We will eat ourselves out of this one,
surely, but not before the blind can see,
our lepers are cleansed, and women give
up what they will.
                    That was another time.
Here, the dead stay dead, with nothing more
required.
          Desire is the cruelest word, and
destination over journey, the creed to follow.
We stuff our mouths, and let tomorrow scrounge
like dogs for itself —
                        We stuff our mouths,
our bellies to a ball, a last supper, the dance
of beggars while the voices sing *hallelujah*
for stockings, for crosses, jump rope and cards.
No heroes, no villains — just a fetish
for the fragmented world
that will not be saved.

   — ***Viridiana*** (1961), Luis Buñuel, dir.

This is not my testament:

cough, moo, the ticking clock — wrenched
inventions of the real — a rolling pin's rub,
drifts of pipe smoke, doors open then close.

Neutrality is blind. Either I am Jesus,
or I am not. And the dead woman will,
in fact, have a successful birthing —

the child will nurse her breast, will have
fat hands and shoulders, his feet will be soft,
always, even though the land is hard

and the field's in need of a certain bruising.
Wind over this field has a simple theology:
grasses move this way or they do not move.

I watch from my window, but I prefer standing
in the middle of the field so the world becomes
a great bird, flying into its perfect bird-life.

    — ***Ordet*** (1955), Carl Theodor Dreyer, dir.

Sam Rasnake's works, receiving five nominations for the Pushcart Prize, have appeared in *OCHO, Wigleaf, Big Muddy, Literal Latté, Poem, Pebble Lake Review, Poets/Artists, New World Writing*, and *Santa Fe Literary Review*, as well as the anthologies **MiPOesias Companion 2012, The Southern Poetry Anthology, Best of the Web 2009, LUMMOX 2012, Flash Fiction Fridays, BOXCAR Poetry Review Anthology 2, Deep River Apartments, The Lost Children**, and **Dogzplot Flash Fiction 2011**. He is the author of **Necessary Motions** (Sow's Ear Press, 1998), **Religions of the Blood** (Pudding House Press, 1998), **Lessons in Morphology** (GOSS183, 2010) and **Inside a Broken Clock** (Finishing Line Press, 2010). He is chapbook editor for *Sow's Ear Poetry Review*, has served as a judge for the Dorothy Sargent Rosenberg Poetry Prize, University of California, Berkeley, and from 2001-2010 was editor of *Blue Fifth Review*. Since 2011, Rasnake has edited, along with Michelle Elvy, the *Blue Five Notebook Series* from *BFR*.

www.ingramcontent.com/pod-product-compliance
Lightning Source LLC
Chambersburg PA
CBHW071735040426
42446CB00012B/2369